PIANO • VOCAL • GUITAR

MOTOWN
50TH ANNIVERSARY SONGBOOK
100 SONGS

YESTERDAY › TODAY › FOREVER

ISBN 978-1-4234-6701-4

HAL•LEONARD®
CORPORATION
7777 W. BLUEMOUND RD. P.O. BOX 13819 MILWAUKEE, WI 53213

Visit Hal Leonard Online at
www.halleonard.com

MOTOWN CELEBRATES THE 50ᵗʰ ANNIVERSARY
OF THE SOUND THAT CHANGED AMERICA

As an irresistible force of social and cultural change, Berry Gordy's legendary Motown Records made its mark not just on the music industry, but society at large, with a sound that has become one of the most significant musical accomplishments and stunning success stories of the 20ᵗʰ century. Diana Ross & the Supremes, Smokey Robinson & the Miracles, Stevie Wonder, the Temptations, the Four Tops, Marvin Gaye, Michael Jackson & the Jackson 5, Lionel Richie & the Commodores, the Marvelettes, Martha Reeves and the Vandellas, Gladys Knight & the Pips, their music communicated and brought together a racially divided country and segregated society, around the world, touching all people of all ages and race. No other record company in history has exerted such an enormous influence on both the style and substance of popular music and culture. With more than 180 No. 1 hit songs worldwide and counting, that influence is still being felt today, from pop to hip-hop, Motown celebrates the 50ᵗʰ anniversary of the company's founding.

Motown, of course, stands for more than just the historic music. The label and its remarkable legacy is a reflection of the hard work of dedicated individuals overcoming incredible obstacles to achieve great success. Nearly a half-century ago, on January 12, 1959, to be exact, a young African-American songwriter named Berry Gordy founded Tamla Records with a loan of $800 from his family, marking the birth of the "Motown Records Corporation." A man of vision, drive, talent, and determination, Berry Gordy was also a producer, innovative entrepreneur, and teacher.

The phenomenal success of Motown Records is a tribute to all that he embodies and all the talent that he brought out in others. Under his leadership, and through determination and support of the Motown family of artists, Gordy forged new grounds for minorities and made the "Motown Sound" a worldwide phenomenon beloved by millions.

Berry Gordy always learned from all his experiences and applied them to his business. He put the tedious time he spent working on the assembly line at Detroit's Lincoln-Mercury automobile plant to good use: "Every day I watched how a bare metal frame, rolling down the line would come off the other end, a spanking brand-new car. What a great idea! Maybe, I could do the same thing with my music. Create a place where a kid off the street could walk in one door, an unknown, go through a process, and come out another door, a star." That little thought that came to him while running up and down that assembly line became a reality we now know as "Motown."

When Motown was housed in its famed "Hitsville U.S.A." offices at 2648 West Grand Boulevard in Detroit, it was not just a location; history would be made there. In fact, Berry Gordy created a twenty-four hour hit-making and artist development factory, nurturing the artistic talent of the singers, writers, producers, as well as, corporate executives. Today, Motown is not only the greatest pop music hit factory ever heard, but an institution, a state of mind, a way of life, a style, the "Sound of Young America." The distinctive, upbeat and uplifting music brought together pop and soul, white and black, old and young, like never before and continues to this day. Regardless of race or social background, teenage girls admired Diana Ross and teenage boys pretended to be Smokey Robinson. Motown became the heartbeat of American pop music. With multi-platinum artists ranging from the Miracles, Temptations, Four Tops and Supremes to Marvin Gaye, Stevie Wonder, and the Jackson 5, the House That Gordy Built had and has no rival. Motown defined the term "crossover" not only on record and stage, but also behind the scenes. After breaking down barriers and having pop radio embrace Motown artists, Berry Gordy set his sights on television. He booked his artists on popular shows such as *American Bandstand* and *The Ed Sullivan Show*, making history as the first African-American artists on these shows. After captivating national audiences with repeat performances on *The Ed Sullivan Show*, the Supremes were the first R&B act to play the country's most prestigious night club, New York's Copacabana, which paved the way for other R&B acts into the top cabaret circuits around the world.

Motown was the first African-American-owned record label to reach widespread national acclaim. Motown broke down racial prejudice by becoming the most successful independent record company in history and the most successful African-American-owned business in America.

After Gordy purchased that first Detroit property, he converted the garage into a small recording studio and the kitchen into the control room. The company's first signing was the Miracles, led by Smokey Robinson, and its first release was Marv Johnson's "Come to Me," January 21, 1959. But its first major hit was Barrett Strong's "Money (That's What I Want)," a song co-written by Gordy himself, which reached #2 on *Billboard's* R&B chart in 1960. A year later, the Miracles would score the company's first million seller with "Shop Around." That same year, teen girl group the Marvelettes landed the company's first pop No. 1, "Please Mr. Postman," while the label signed two young groups, the Supremes and the Temptations. Within three years, those two groups would lead Motown into

the mainstream, when the Supremes launched an unprecedented string of five consecutive No. 1 hits, starting with "Where Did Our Love Go," while the Temptations released the eternal Motown classic, "My Girl." In 1968 the company had five records out of the Top 10 on *Billboard's* Hot 100 chart and accomplished another unprecedented feat by seizing the top three spots for a full month.

Upon his induction into the Rock and Roll Hall of Fame in 1988, Motown's founder was given the following tribute:

> "Gordy endeavored to reach across the racial divide with music that could touch all people, regardless of the color of their skin. Under his tutelage, Motown became a model of black capitalism, pride and self-expression and a repository for some of the greatest talent ever assembled at one company . . . Motown's stable of singers, songwriters, producers and musicians took the concept of simple, catchy pop songs to a whole new level of sophistication and, thanks to the music's roots in gospel and blues, visceral intensity . . . After Motown, black popular music would never again be dismissed as a minority taste. . . . Aesthetically no less than commercially, Motown's achievements will likely remain unrivaled and untoppable."

Today, the label is part of the Universal Music Group, with its classic recorded music catalog managed by Universal Music Enterprises (UMe). The timeless songs from Motown between 1959 and 1985 are represented by EMI Music Publishing.

From late 2008 to the end of 2009, Universal Music Group and EMI Music Publishing will mark the historic Detroit label's musical achievements with a series of initiatives. Notably, Universal Music Enterprises will issue monthly music releases in both physical and digital formats, with bonus tracks enhancing these packages. Details will be announced as each new package approaches.

Also upcoming throughout the celebration are releases of classic Motown television specials in a series of DVD collections and *Inside Motown,* a multi-part documentary on how the company was built.

ABC

Words and Music by ALPHONSO MIZELL,
FREDERICK PERREN, DEKE RICHARDS and BERRY GORDY

With drive

Buh, buh, buh, buh, buh, boo, buh, buh, buh, buh, buh, buh. You

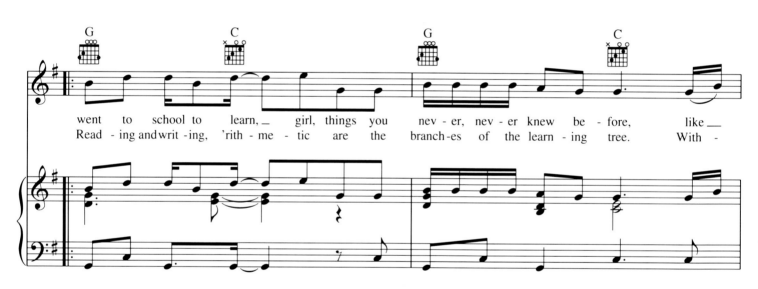

went to school to learn, _ girl, things you nev - er, nev - er knew be - fore, like _
Read - ing and writ - ing, 'rith - me - tic are the branch - es of the learn - ing tree. With -

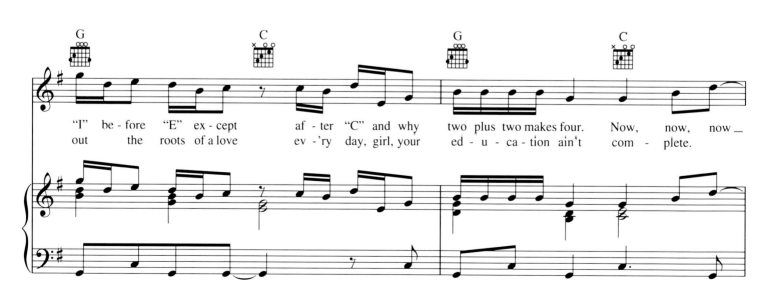

"I" be - fore "E" ex - cept af - ter "C" and why two plus two makes four. Now, now, now _
out the roots of a love ev - 'ry day, girl, your ed - u - ca - tion ain't com - plete.

Bass Vamp

Ain't No Mountain High Enough

Words and Music by NICKOLAS ASHFORD
and VALERIE SIMPSON

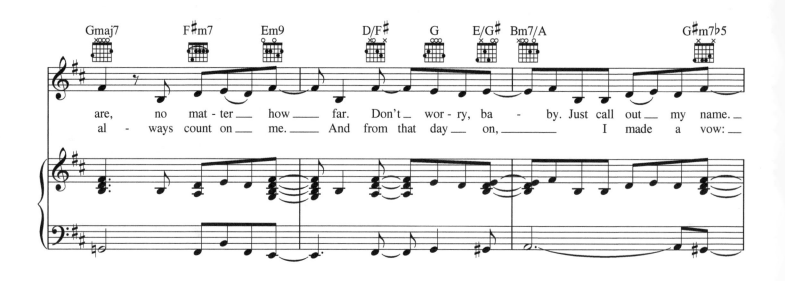

Repeat and Fade

AIN'T NOTHING LIKE THE REAL THING

Words and Music by NICKOLAS ASHFORD
and VALERIE SIMPSON

Moderately

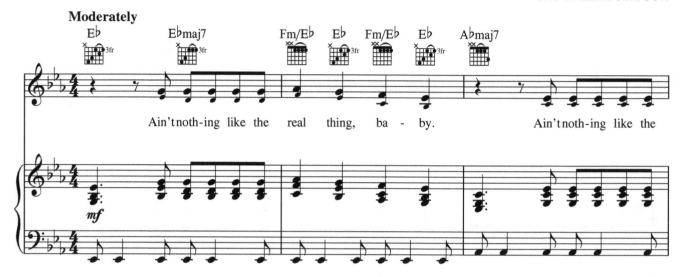

Ain't noth-ing like the real thing, ba - by. Ain't noth-ing like the

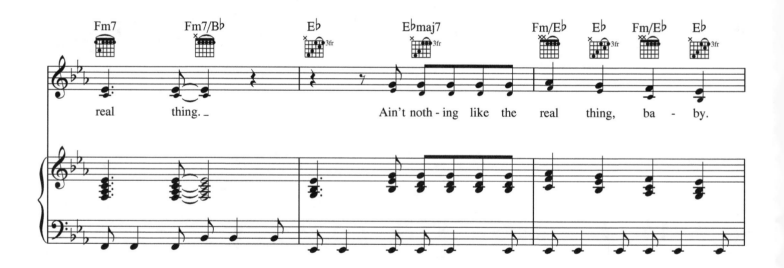

real thing. _ Ain't noth-ing like the real thing, ba - by.

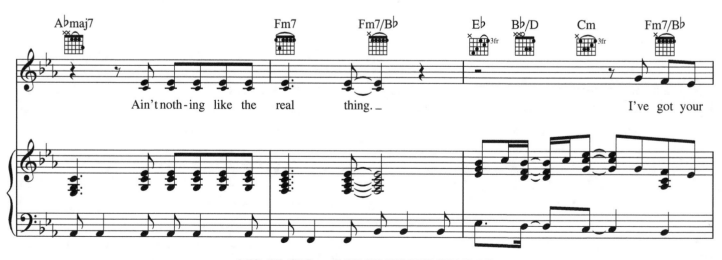

Ain't noth-ing like the real thing. _ I've got your

AIN'T TOO PROUD TO BEG

Words and Music by EDWARD HOLLAND
and NORMAN WHITFIELD

Moderately fast

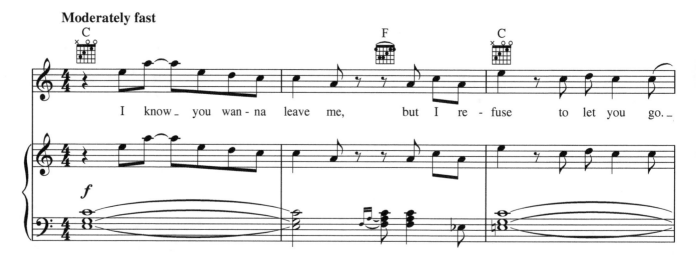

I know you wan-na leave me, but I re-fuse to let you go.

If I have to beg, plead for your sym-pa-thy, I don't mind

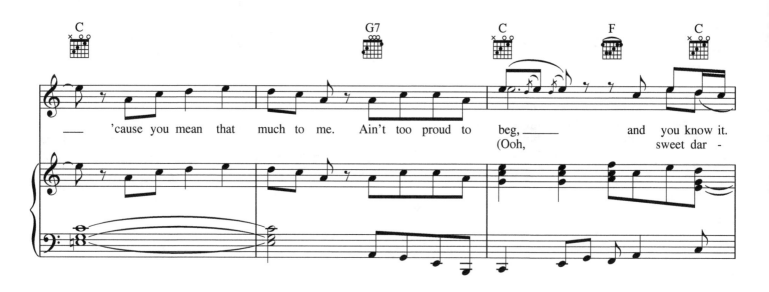

'cause you mean that much to me. Ain't too proud to beg, and you know it.
(Ooh, sweet dar -

ALL NIGHT LONG
(All Night)

Words and Music by
LIONEL RICHIE

long. _____ Ev -'ry - one _ you meet, _ they're

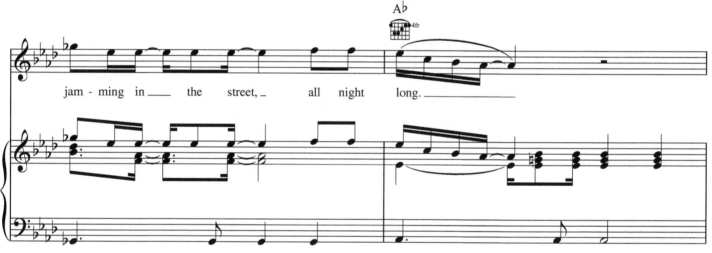

jam - ming in _____ the street, _ all night long. _____

Repeat and Fade   **Optional Ending**

BABY LOVE

Words and Music by BRIAN HOLLAND,
EDWARD HOLLAND and LAMONT DOZIER

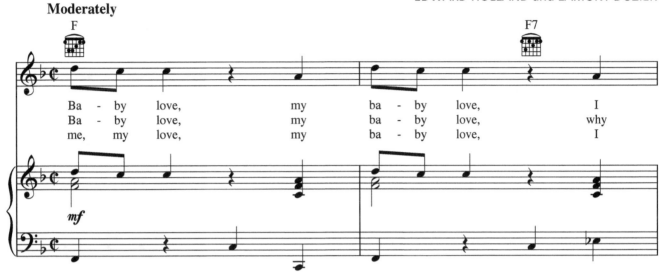

Baby love, my baby love, I
Baby love, my baby love, why
me, my love, my baby love, I

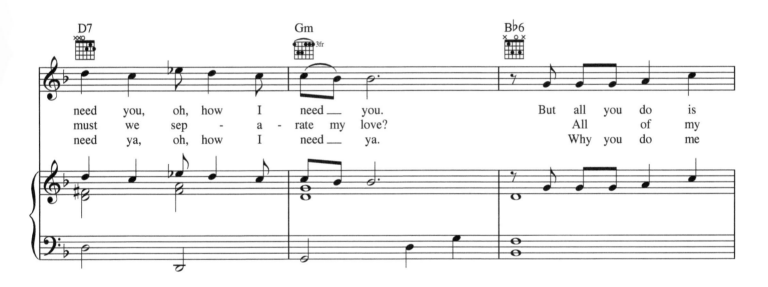

need you, oh, how I need you.
must we sep-a-rate my love?
need ya, oh, how I need ya.

But all you do is
All of my
Why you do me

treat me bad, break my heart and leave me sad.
whole life through, I nev-er love no one but you.
like you do, af-ter I've been true to you?

BABY I NEED YOUR LOVIN'

Words and Music by BRIAN HOLLAND,
LAMONT DOZIER and EDWARD HOLLAND

BACK IN MY ARMS AGAIN

Words and Music by BRIAN HOLLAND,
LAMONT DOZIER and EDWARD HOLLAND

1. All day long I hear my tel - e - phone ring, friends
2. ea - sy for friends to say let him go, but
3. *(See additional lyrics)*

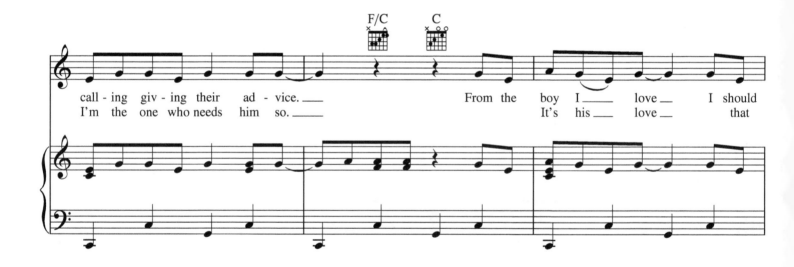

call - ing giv - ing their ad - vice. ___ From the boy I ___ love ___ I should
I'm the one who needs him so. ___ It's his ___ love ___ that

break a - way ___ 'cause heart - aches he'll bring one day. ___
makes me strong; ___ with - out him I can't go on. ___

Additional Lyrics

3. How can Mary tell me what to do
When she lost her love so true;
And Flo, she don't know
'Cause the boy she loves is a Romeo.
I listened once to my friends' advice
But it's not gonna happen twice.
'Cause all the advice ever's gotten me
Was many long and sleepless nights. Oo!
I got him back in my arms again.
Right by my side.
I got him back in my arms again,
So satisfied. *(Fade)*

BALL OF CONFUSION
(That's What the World Is Today)

Words and Music by NORMAN WHITFIELD
and BARRETT STRONG

Peo-ple mov-in' out, peo-ple mov-in' in, why?___ Be - cause of the col - or of their skin,

run, run, run ___ but you sho' can't hide. ___ An

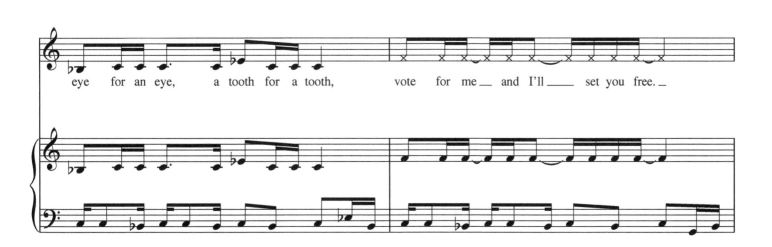

eye for an eye, a tooth for a tooth, vote for me ___ and I'll ___ set you free. ___

46

Rap on, _____ broth - er, rap on. ____ Well, _____ the on - ly per - son talk - in' 'bout love thy broth - er is the preach - er, and it seems no - bod - y's in - ter - est - ed in learn - ing but the teach - er. Seg - re - ga - tion, de - ter - mi - na - tion, dem - on - stra - tion, in - te - gra - tion, ag - gra - va - tion, hu - mil - i - a - tion, ob - li - ga - tion to our na - tion,

ball of con-fu - sion, __ oh __ yeah, __ that's what the world is to-day.

The sale of pills __ is at an all - time high,

young folks walk-in' 'round __ with their heads in the sky, __ cit-ies a - flame __ in the sum-mer-time, __ and, oh, __

_____ the beat goes on. __

48

Ev-o-lu-tion, rev-o-lu-tion, gun con-trol, the sound of soul, shoot-in' rock-ets to the moon, kids grow-ing up too soon.

Pol-i-ti-cians say more tax-es will solve ev-'ry-thing, and the band played

on.

Round and a-round and a-round we go where the world's head-ed no-bod-y knows.

Great goo - ga moo - ga can't you hear me talk - in' to you just a

ball of con - fu - sion. _____ Oh ____ yeah, ____

that's what the world is ____ to - day. ____

BEAUTY IS ONLY SKIN DEEP

Words and Music by EDWARD HOLLAND
and NORMAN WHITFIELD

BEECHWOOD 4-5789

Words and Music by MARVIN GAYE,
WILLIAM STEVENSON and GEORGE GORDY

Moderately fast Rock

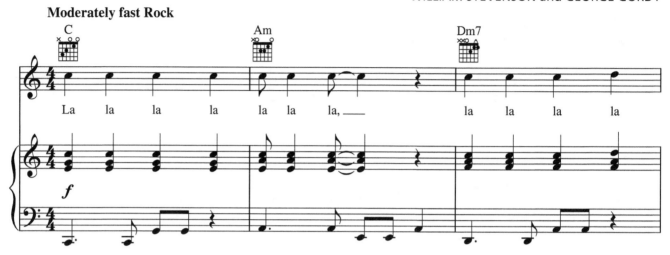

La la la la la la la, ___ la la la la

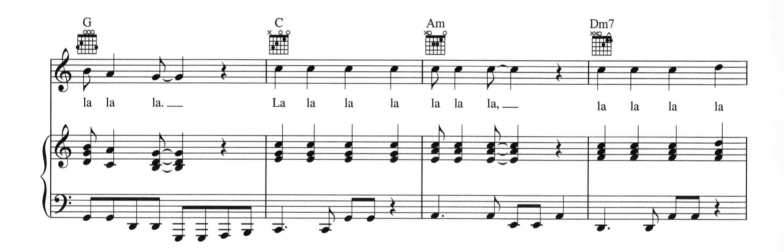

la la la. ___ La la la la la la la, ___ la la la la

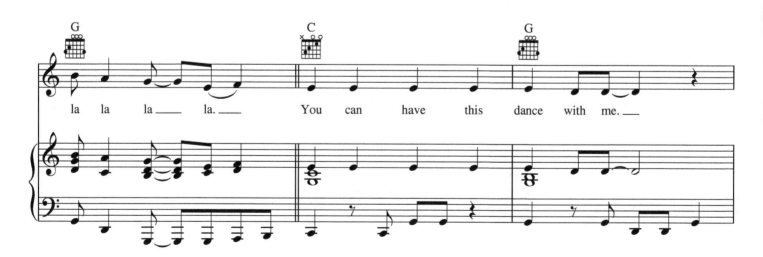

la la la ___ la. ___ You can have this dance with me. ___

BEING WITH YOU

Words and Music by
WILLIAM "SMOKEY" ROBINSON

I don't care what they think ___ a - bout me, and ___
I don't care if they start ___ to a - void me;

I don't care what they say. ___
I don't care what they do. ___

I don't care what they think ___
I don't care a - bout an -

*Optional repeat of 8 bar Intro. (Instr. solo) before 2nd Verse.

64

BERNADETTE

Words and Music by BRIAN HOLLAND,
LAMONT DOZIER and EDWARD HOLLAND

BEN

Words by DON BLACK
Music by WALTER SCHARF

BRICK HOUSE

Words and Music by LIONEL RICHIE, RONALD LaPREAD,
WALTER ORANGE, MILAN WILLIAMS,
THOMAS McCLARY and WILLIAM KING

COME SEE ABOUT ME

Words and Music by LAMONT DOZIER,
BRIAN HOLLAND and EDWARD HOLLAND

CRUISIN'

Words and Music by WILLIAM "SMOKEY" ROBINSON
and MARVIN TARPLIN

Moderately slow

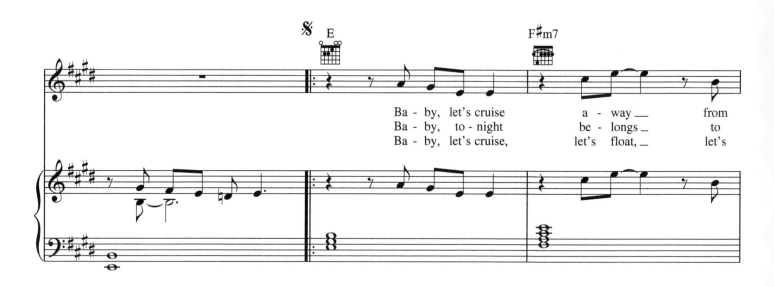

Ba - by, let's cruise   a - way   from
Ba - by, to - night   be - longs   to
Ba - by, let's cruise,   let's float,   let's

here.   Don't be con - fused,   the way   is
us.   Ev - 'ry - thing's right,   do what   you
glide.   Let's o - pen love   and go   in -

DANCING IN THE STREET

Words and Music by MARVIN GAYE,
IVY HUNTER and WILLIAM STEVENSON

Moderately, with a steady beat

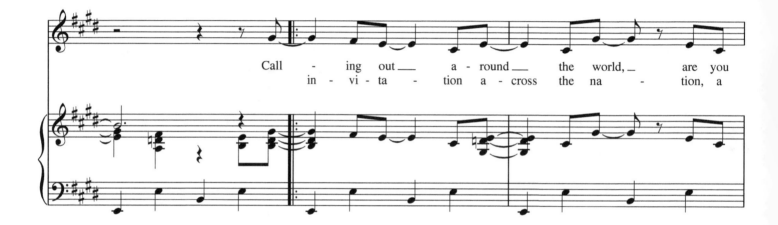

Call - ing out __ a - round __ the world, __ are you
in - vi - ta - tion a - cross the na - tion, a

read - y for a brand-new beat? __ Sum - mer's here __ and the
chance for folks to meet. __ There'll be laugh - ing, sing - ing __ and

time is right __ for danc - ing in the street. __ They're danc - ing in Chi -
mu - sic swing - ing, danc - ing in the street. __ Phil - a - del - phia, P. A.,

DO YOU KNOW WHERE YOU'RE GOING TO?

Theme from MAHOGANY

Words by GERRY GOFFIN
Music by MICHAEL MASSER

96

Now ___ look - ing back at all ___ we planned,

we let ___ so man - y dreams ___ just slip through our ___ hands. ___

DO YOU LOVE ME

Words and Music by
BERRY GORDY

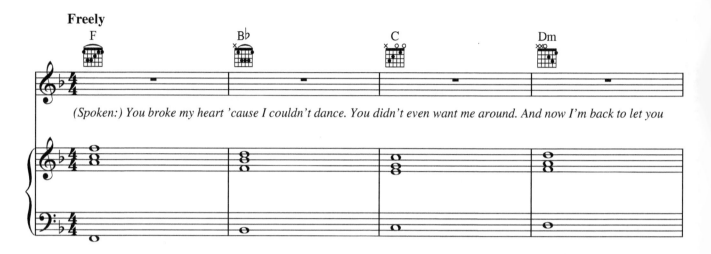

(Spoken:) You broke my heart 'cause I couldn't dance. You didn't even want me around. And now I'm back to let you

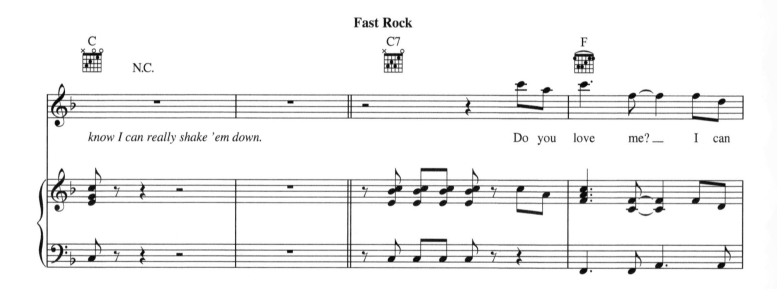

know I can really shake 'em down. Do you love me?__ I can

real-ly move.__ Do you love me?__ I'm in the groove.__ Now do you

EASY

Words and Music by
LIONEL RICHIE

END OF THE ROAD
from the Paramount Motion Picture BOOMERANG

Words and Music by BABYFACE,
L.A. REID and DARYL SIMMONS

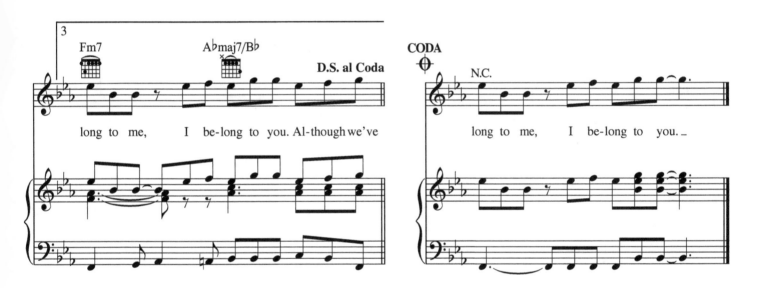

Additional Lyrics

(Spoken:) *Girl, I'm here for you.*
All those times at night when you just hurt me,
And just ran out with that other fellow,
Baby, I knew about it.
I just didn't care.
You just don't understand how much I love you, do you?
I'm here for you.
I'm not out to go out there and cheat all night just like you did, baby.
But that's alright, huh, I love you anyway.
And I'm still gonna be here for you 'til my dyin' day, baby.
Right now, I'm just in so much pain, baby.
'Cause you just won't come back to me, will you?
Just come back to me.

Yes, baby, my heart is lonely.
My heart hurts, baby, yes, I feel pain too.
Baby, please...

ENDLESS LOVE

Words and Music by
LIONEL RICHIE

Oh, _____ and _____ love, _____

FINGERTIPS
(Part 2)

Words and Music by CLARENCE O. PAUL
and HENRY COSBY

Moderately fast

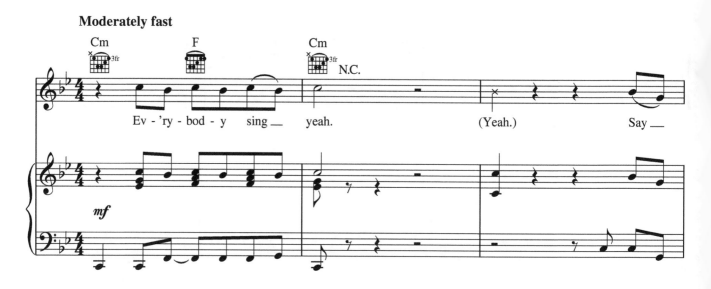

Solo ends I know that I nev - er gon - na hey, yeah. __ Ev - 'ry -

FOR ONCE IN MY LIFE

Words by RONALD MILLER
Music by ORLANDO MURDEN

GET READY

Words and Music by
WILLIAM "SMOKEY" ROBINSON

Moderately, with a beat

nev-er met a girl who makes __ me feel __ the way that
wan-na play __ hide and seek __ with love, __ let me re-
All __ my __ friends should-n't want me to, __ I un-der-

you do. (It's al - right.) __ When-ev-er I'm asked __ who makes
mind you. (It's al - right.) __ The lov-ing you're gon - na miss,
stand it. (Be al - right.) __ I hope __ I'll get __ to you be-

HEATWAVE
(Love Is Like a Heatwave)

Words and Music by EDWARD HOLLAND,
LAMONT DOZIER and BRIAN HOLLAND

Moderately fast

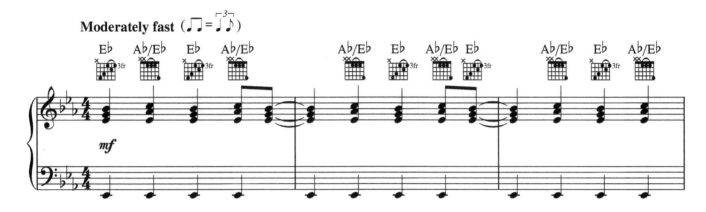

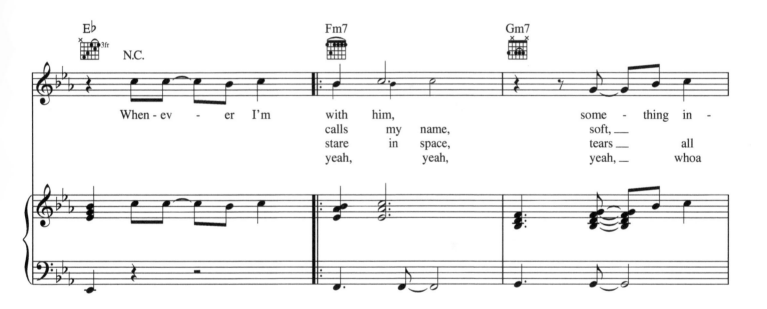

When-ev-er I'm with him,
calls my name,
stare in space,
yeah, yeah,

some-thing in-
soft, ___
tears ___ all
yeah, ___ whoa

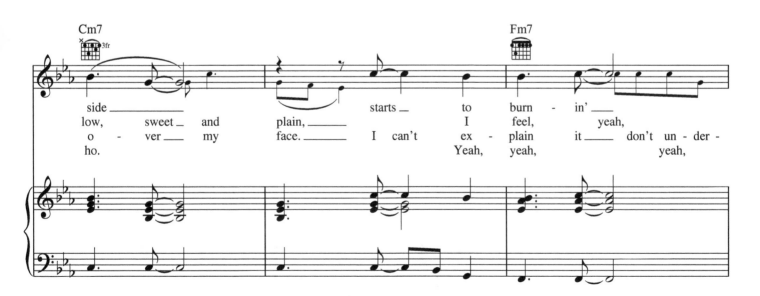

side ___
low, sweet ___ and
o-ver ___ my
ho.

starts ___ to burn-in'
plain, ___ I feel, yeah,
face. ___ I can't ex-plain it ___ don't un-der-
Yeah, yeah, yeah,

yeah, and __ I'm filled with __ de - sire. __ Has
stand it, I ain't nev - er felt like this be - fore. Now
yeah, ho, yeah.

Could it be a dev - il in me __ or is this the way __ love's sup-
high blood pres-sure got a hold on me __ or is this the way __ love's sup-
that fun - ny feel - in' has me a - mazed; __ I don't know what to __ do, my
Don't pass up this chance; __ this time __ it's a

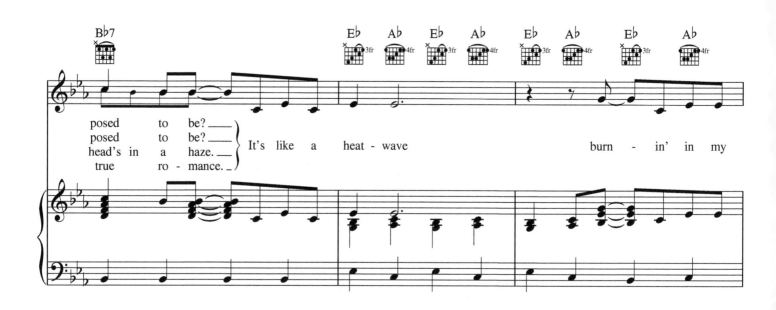

posed to be? __
posed to be? __
head's in a haze. __ } It's like a heat - wave burn - in' in my
true ro - mance. __

GOING TO A GO-GO

Words and Music by WILLIAM "SMOKEY" ROBINSON,
MARVIN TARPLIN, WARREN MOORE and ROBERT ROGERS

GOT TO BE THERE

Words and Music by
ELLIOTT WILLENSKY

So, I've got to be there,__ got to be there__ in the morn-
That's why I've got to be there,__ got to be there_____ where love__

-ing, and wel-come {her}{him} in - to my world, ___ and
___ be-gins and that's ev-'ry-where__ {she}{he} goes; ___ I've

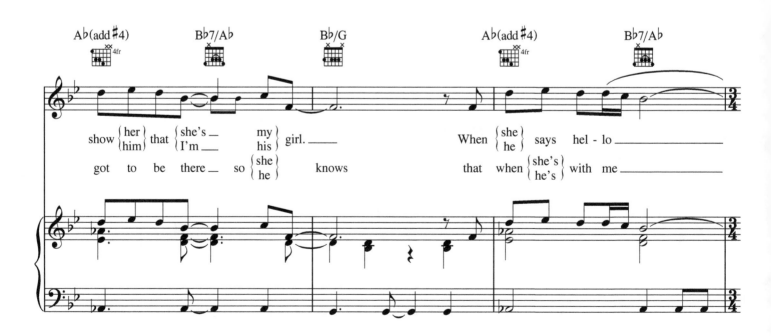

show {her}{him} that {she's__}{I'm__} {my}{his} girl. ___ When {she}{he} says hel-lo _____
got to be there__ so {she}{he} knows that when {she's}{he's} with me _____

THE HAPPENING

Words and Music by LAMONT DOZIER, EDWARD HOLLAND JR.,
BRIAN HOLLAND and FRANK DEVOL

147

Additional Lyrics

3. So sure I felt secure
   Until love took a detour;
   'Cause when you got a tender love
   You don't take care of,
   Then you better beware of   (Fade)

HOW SWEET IT IS
(To Be Loved by You)

Words and Music by EDWARD HOLLAND,
LAMONT DOZIER and BRIAN HOLLAND

Moderate, with a shuffle

HELLO

Words and Music by
LIONEL RICHIE

Slow Ballad

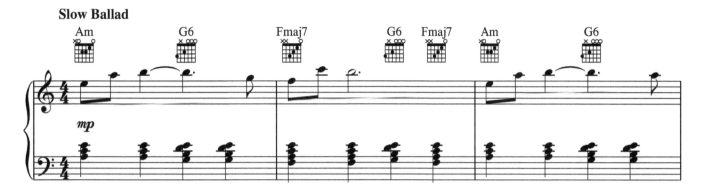

I've been a - lone with you in - side my ___ mind ___ and
long to see the sun - light in your ___ hair ___ and

Instrumental solo

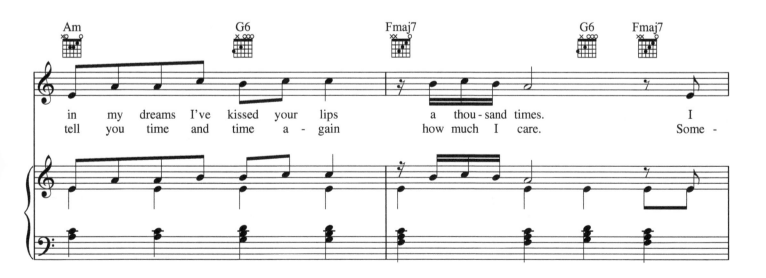

in my dreams I've kissed your lips a thou - sand times. I
tell you time and time a - gain how much I care. Some -

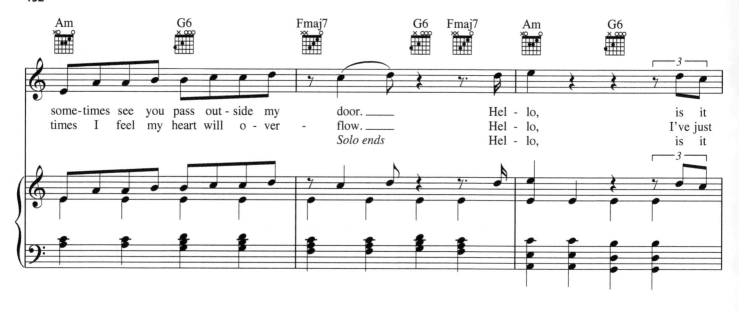

HIGHER GROUND

Words and Music by
STEVIE WONDER

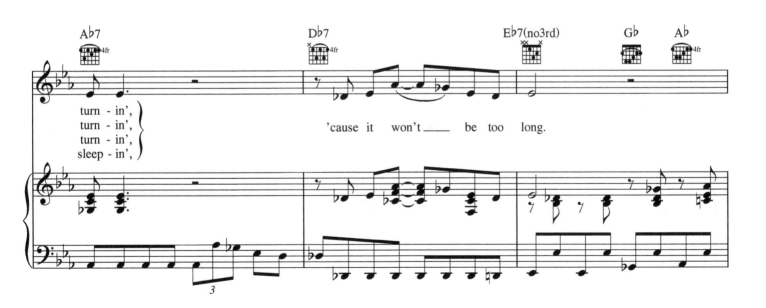

I CAN'T GET NEXT TO YOU

Words and Music by BARRETT STRONG
and NORMAN WHITFIELD

Additional Lyrics

2. I can fly like a bird in the sky
   And I can buy anything that money can buy.
   I can turn a river into a raging fire.
   I can live forever if I so desire.
   I don't want it, all these things I can do
   'Cause I can't get next to you.
   Chorus

3. I can turn back the hands of time — you better believe I can.
   I can make the seasons change just by waving my hand.
   I can change anything from old to new.
   The thing I want to do the most I'm unable to do.
   I'm an unhappy woman with all the powers I possess
   'Cause man, you're the key to my happiness.

I CAN'T HELP MYSELF
(Sugar Pie, Honey Bunch)

Words and Music by BRIAN HOLLAND,
LAMONT DOZIER and EDWARD HOLLAND

Sug-ar pie, hon-ey bunch, you know that I
Sug-ar pie, hon-ey bunch, I'm weak-er than a

love you. _____ I can't help my-self,
man should be. I can't help my-self,

I HEAR A SYMPHONY

Words and Music by EDWARD HOLLAND,
LAMONT DOZIER and BRIAN HOLLAND

I'LL BE THERE

Words and Music by BERRY GORDY, HAL DAVIS,
WILLIE HUTCH and BOB WEST

I HEARD IT THROUGH THE GRAPEVINE

Words and Music by NORMAN J. WHITFIELD
and BARRETT STRONG

I JUST CALLED TO SAY I LOVE YOU

Words and Music by
STEVIE WONDER

Additional Lyrics

3. No summer's high; no warm July;
   No harvest moon to light one tender August night.
   No autumn breeze; no falling leaves;
   Not even time for birds to fly to southern skies.

4. No Libra sun; no Halloween;
   No giving thanks to all the Christmas joy you bring.
   But what it is, though old so new
   To fill your heart like no three words could ever do.
   Chorus

I SECOND THAT EMOTION

Words and Music by WILLIAM "SMOKEY" ROBINSON
and ALFRED CLEVELAND

I WANT YOU BACK

Words and Music by FREDDIE PERREN,
ALPHONSO MIZELL, BERRY GORDY and DEKE RICHARDS

I WAS MADE TO LOVE HER

Words and Music by STEVIE WONDER,
LULA MAE HARDAWAY, SYLVIA MOY
and HENRY COSBY

I WISH

Words and Music by
STEVIE WONDER

Looking back on when _____ I was a lit - tle nap - py - head - ed boy. _
Broth - er says he's tell - in' 'bout you play - in' doc - tor with _ that girl. _

I'M GONNA MAKE YOU LOVE ME

Words and Music by LEON HUFF,
KENNETH GAMBLE and JERRY ROSS

IF I WERE YOUR WOMAN

Words and Music by CLAY McMURRAY,
PAMELA SAWYER and GLORIA JONES

Moderate Ballad, with a beat

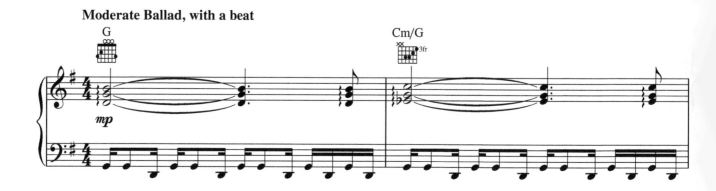

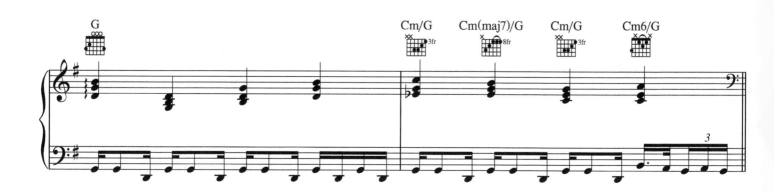

If I were your wom-an _____ and you were my man,

D.S. al Coda

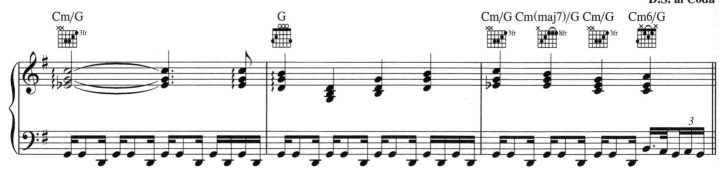

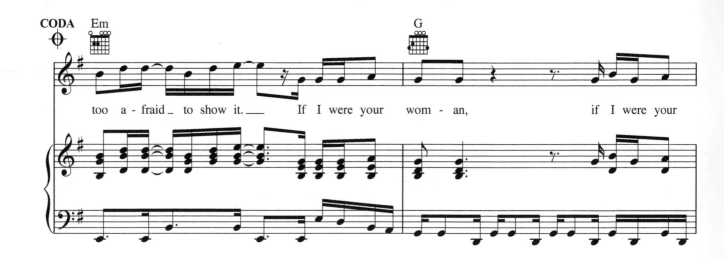

too a-fraid_ to show it.___ If I were your wom - an, if I were your

wom - an, if I were your wom - an, here's_ what I'd

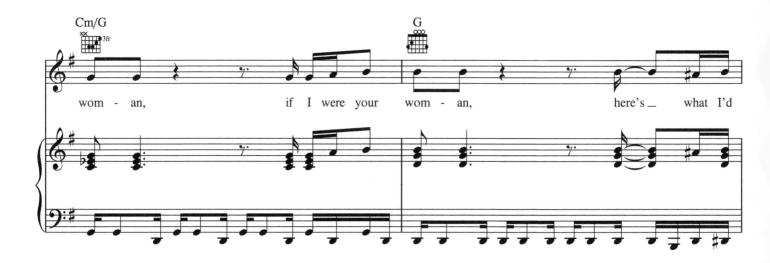

do;_____ I'd nev - er, no,_ no, no, stop lov - ing

INNER CITY BLUES
(Makes Me Wanna Holler)

Words and Music by MARVIN GAYE
and JAMES NYX

Dah dah dah dah ___ dah   dah ___ dah dah   dah dah ___   dah dah dah.

Rock - ets ___   and moon - shots
- tion ___   no   chance   to ___

spend it on ___   the have nots,   mon - ey ___   we   make ___
___ in-crease ___   fi - nance   bills ___ pile up ___   sky ___

Recorded a half step lower.

216

ISN'T SHE LOVELY

Words and Music by
STEVIE WONDER

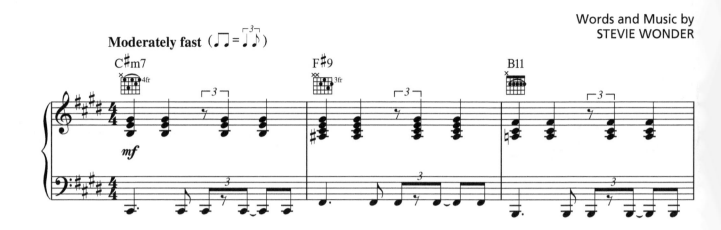

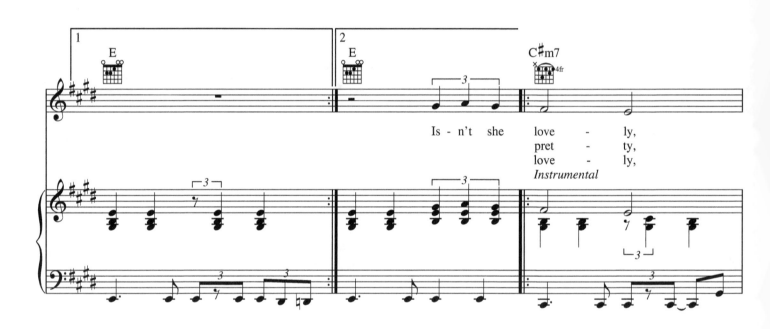

Is - n't she love - ly,
pret - ty,
love - ly,
Instrumental

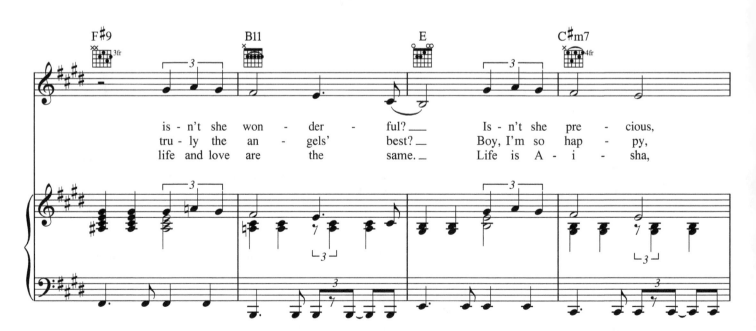

is - n't she won - der - ful? ___ Is - n't she pre - cious,
tru - ly the an - gels' best? ___ Boy, I'm so hap - py,
life and love are the same. ___ Life is A - i - sha,

less than one min - ute old? _____ I nev - er thought _ through love we'd be _____
we have been heav - en blessed. _____ I can't be - lieve _____ what God has done, _____
the mean-ing of her name. _____ Lon - die, it could _____ have not been done _____

_____ mak - ing one as love - ly _____ as she. _____ But is - n't she love - ly,
_____ through us He's giv - en life _____ to one. _____ But is - n't she love - ly,
_____ with - out you who con - ceived _ the one. _____ That's so ver - y love - ly,

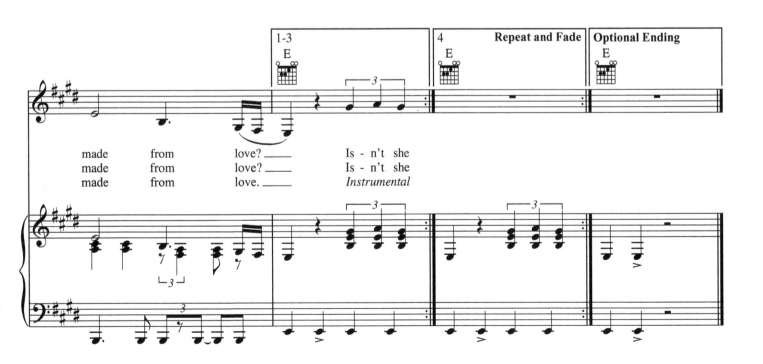

made from love? _____ Is - n't she
made from love? _____ Is - n't she
made from love. _____ *Instrumental*

JIMMY MACK

Words and Music by BRIAN HOLLAND,
LAMONT DOZIER and EDWARD HOLLAND

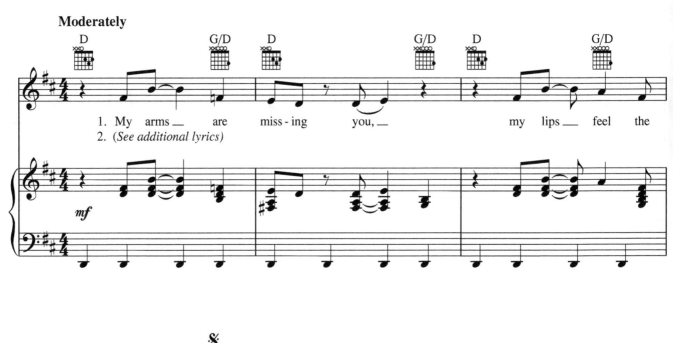

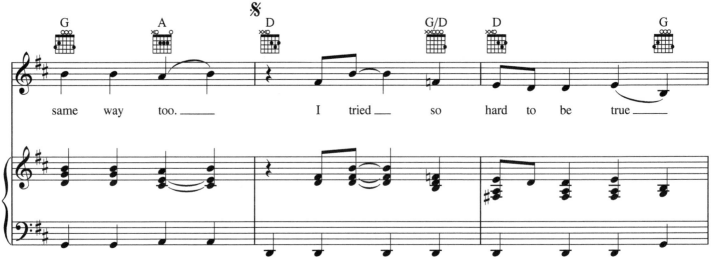

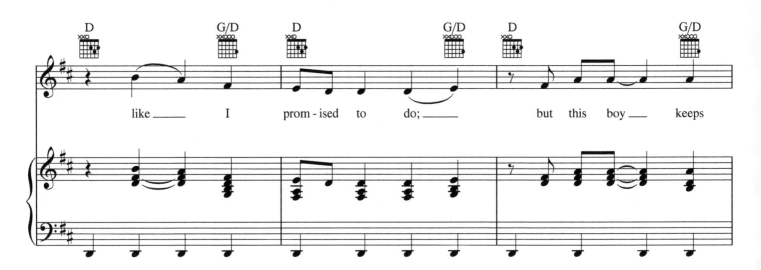

Additional Lyrics

2. He calls me on the phone about three times a day
   Now my heart's just listening to what he has to say.
   But this loneliness I have within
   Keeps reaching out to be his friend.
   Hey, Jimmy, Jimmy oh Jimmy Mack,
   When are you coming back?
   Jimmy, Jimmy oh Jimmy Mack, you better hurry back.

JUST MY IMAGINATION
(Running Away with Me)

Words and Music by NORMAN J. WHITFIELD
and BARRETT STRONG

Each day through my win-dow I watch her as she pass-es by. I
Soon we'll be mar-ried and raise a fam-i-ly.

say to my-self, "You're such a luck-y guy.
A co-zy lit-tle home out in the coun-try with two chil-dren, may-be three.

LET'S GET IT ON

Words and Music by MARVIN GAYE
and ED TOWNSEND

Slow Soul beat

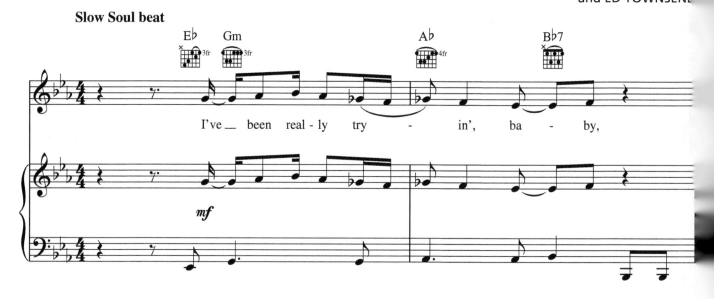

I've been real-ly try-in', ba - by,

try-in' to hold back this feel-in' for so long. And if you feel

like I feel, ba-by, then come on, on, come on. Ooh, let's get it

LOVE CHILD

Words and Music by DEKE RICHARDS,
PAMELA SAWYER, DEAN R. TAYLOR
and FRANK E. WILSON

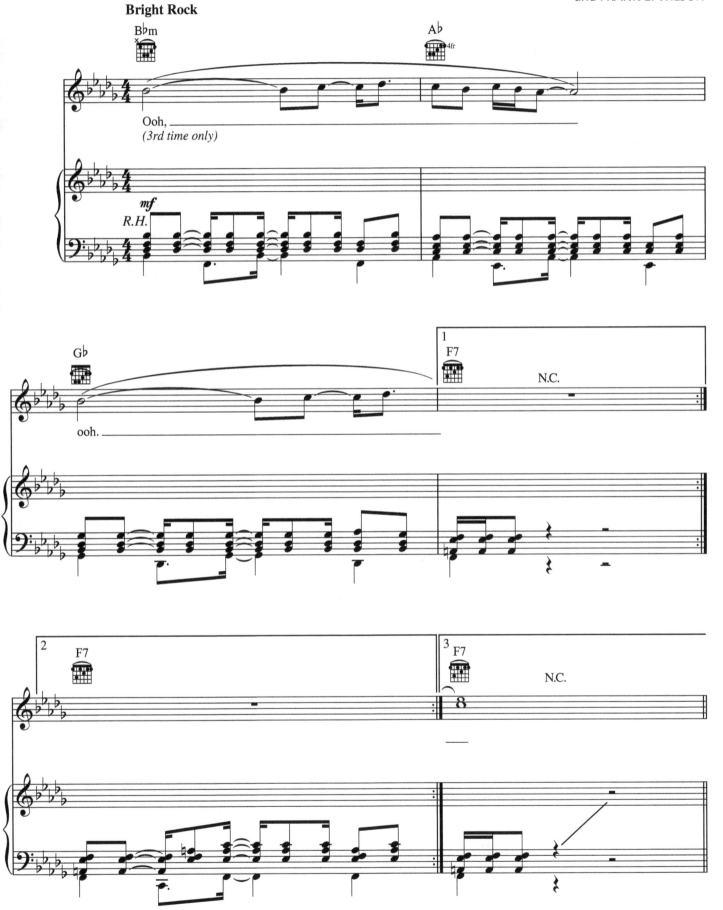

-ed my life _____ in an old, cold run - down _ ten-
-ed school _____ in a worn, torn dress that _ some - bod-

- e - ment slum. My fa - ther left, _ he nev - er e - ven mar-
- y threw out. I knew _ the way _ it was _ to al - ways live

- ried mom. _ They shared the guilt _ my mom - ma knew, _ so a - fraid _ that oth-
_ in doubt, _ to be with - out _ the sim - ple things, _ so a - fraid _ my friends _

- ers knew _ I had _ no _____ name. _____
_ could see _ the guilt _ in _____ me. _

LOVE HANGOVER

Words and Music by MARILYN McLEOD
and PAMELA SAWYER

Moderately slow

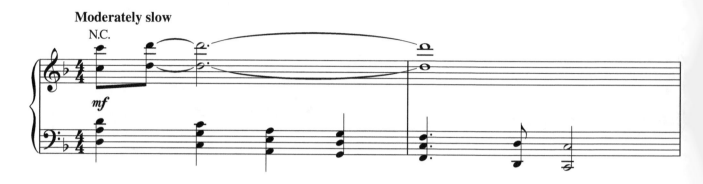

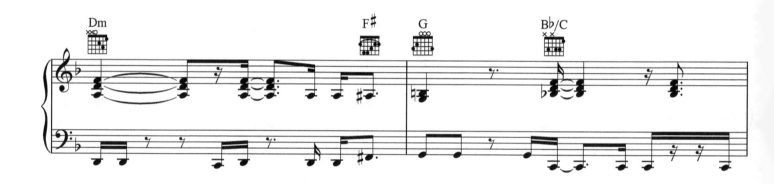

If there's a cure for this, __ I don't want __ it, don't want __ it.
If there's a cure for this, __ I don't want __ it, don't want __ it.

THE LOVE YOU SAVE

Words and Music by BERRY GORDY,
ALPHONSO MIZELL, FREDDIE PERREN
and DENNIS LUSSIER

252

LOVE IS HERE
AND NOW YOU'RE GONE

Words and Music by BRIAN HOLLAND,
LAMONT DOZIER and EDWARD HOLLAND JR.

258

MERCY, MERCY ME
(The Ecology)

Words and Music by
MARVIN GAYE

MY CHERIE AMOUR

Words and Music by STEVIE WONDER,
SYLVIA MOY and HENRY COSBY

dis - tant as the Milk - y Way. _____ My Che -
nev - er no - ticed me. _____ My Che -
share your lit - tle dis - tant cloud. _____ Oh, Che -

rie A - mour, _ pret - ty lit - tle one that I _____ a - dore, _
rie A - mour, _ won't you tell me how could you _____ ig - nore _
rie A - mour, _ pret - ty lit - tle one that I _____ a - dore, _

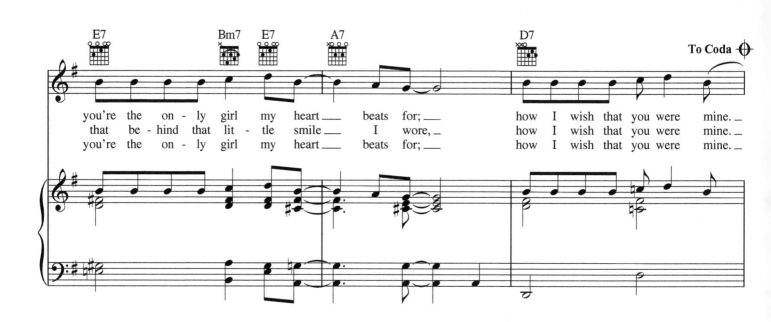

you're the on - ly girl my heart ___ beats for; ___ how I wish that you were mine. _
that be - hind that lit - tle smile ___ I wore, _ how I wish that you were mine. _
you're the on - ly girl my heart ___ beats for; ___ how I wish that you were mine. _

To Coda

MONEY
(That's What I Want)

Words and Music by BERRY GORDY
and JANIE BRADFORD

Moderate Rock

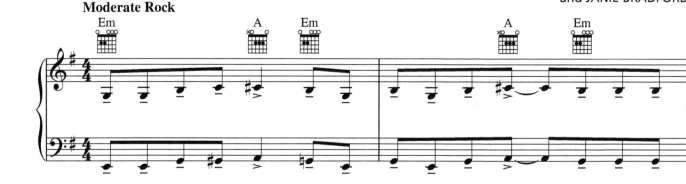

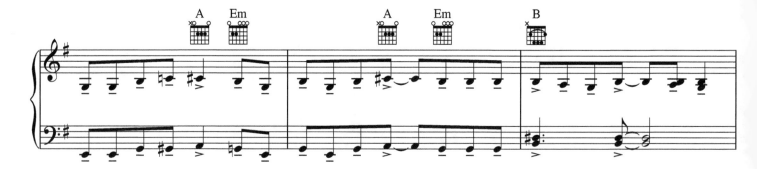

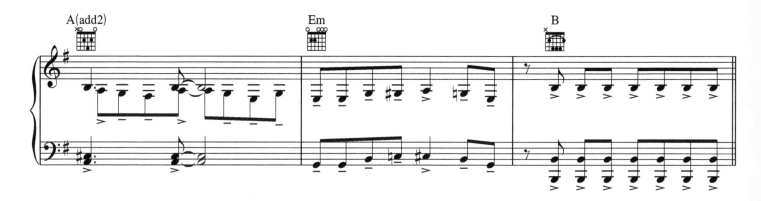

(1.) The best ___ things in life are free, ___
(2.) Your lov - in' give me a thrill, ___
(3,4.) Mon - ey don't get ev - 'ry - thing it's true, ___

but you can keep 'em for the birds and bees; Now give me
but your lov - in' don't pay my bills;
what it don't get I can't use;

That's   what I want.   That's
mon - ey,   that's what I want,

what I want.   That's   what I   want,
that's what I   want,   yeah,

MORE LOVE

Words and Music by
WILLIAM "SMOKEY" ROBINSON

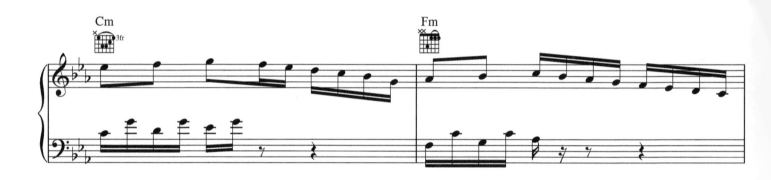

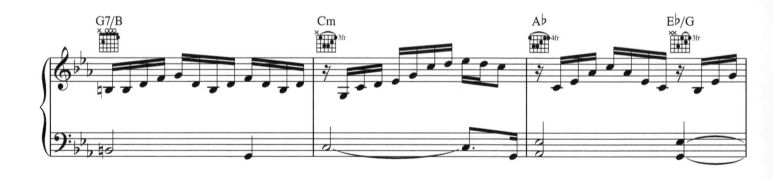

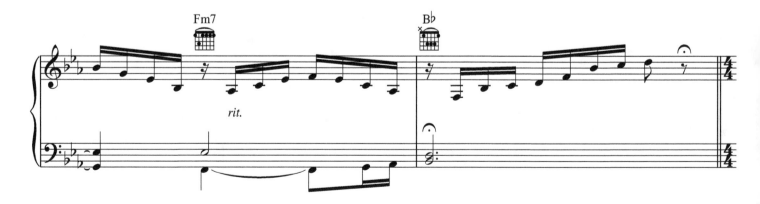

MY GIRL

Words and Music by WILLIAM "SMOKEY" ROBINSON
and RONALD WHITE

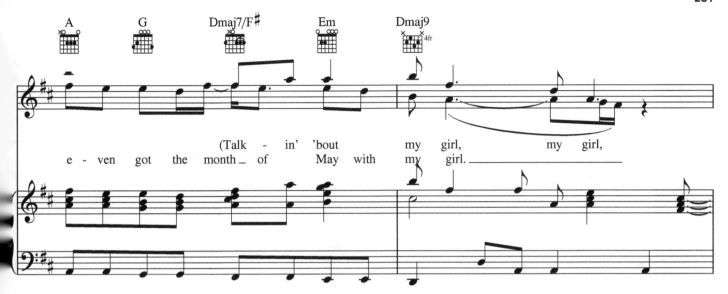

(Talk - in' 'bout   my   girl,   my girl,
e - ven got the month _ of   May with my   girl. _____

my   girl,   whoa, ___ whoa.) _____
Talk - in' 'bout, _ talk - in' 'bout,   talk - in' 'bout _ my ____ girl. _____

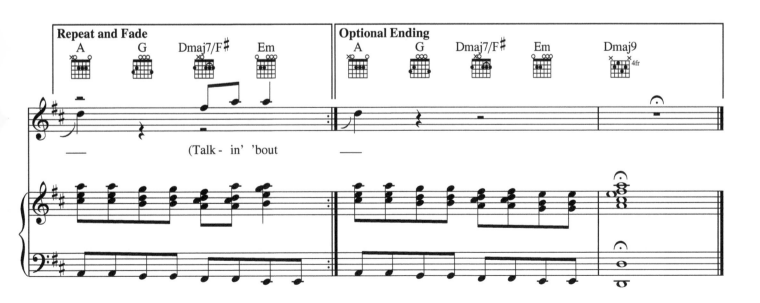

(Talk - in' 'bout

MY GUY

Words and Music by
WILLIAM "SMOKEY" ROBINSON

NEVER CAN SAY GOODBYE

Words and Music by
CLIFTON DAVIS

NEITHER ONE OF US
(Wants to Be the First to Say Goodbye)

Words and Music by
JIM WEATHERLY

OOO BABY BABY

Words and Music by WILLIAM "SMOKEY" ROBINSON
and WARREN MOORE

Slowly

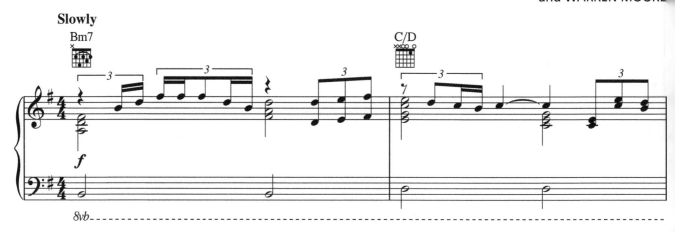

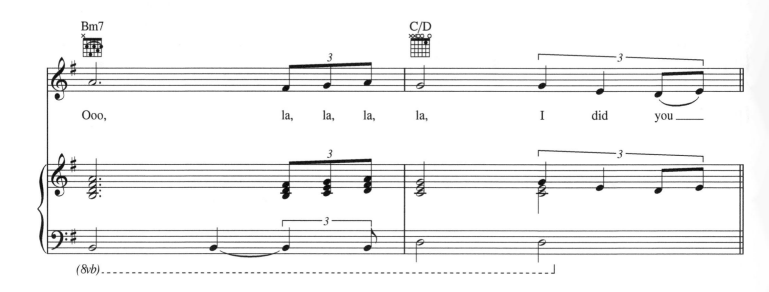

Ooo, la, la, la, la, I did you

wrong; ___ my heart ___ went out to play, and in the game, ___ I
takes, ___ I know ___ I've made a few, but I'm on - ly

PAPA WAS A ROLLIN' STONE

Words and Music by NORMAN WHITFIELD
and BARRETT STRONG

It was the third of Sep - tem - ber.

nev - er got a chance to see ___ him.

That day I'll al - ways re - mem - ber, yes, I will, ___ 'cause

___ him. Nev - er heard noth - in' but bad things a - bout him.

that was the day ___ that my dad - dy died. _____
Ma - ma, I'm de - pend - ing on you to tell me the truth. _

I ___ *(Spoken:) Mama just hung her head and said, "Son,*

Pa - pa was a roll - in' stone." _ Wher - ev - er he laid his hat

was his home. _ And when he died, _ all ___ he ___ left us was a -

PLEASE MR. POSTMAN

Words and Music by ROBERT BATEMAN,
GEORGIA DOBBINS, WILLIAM GARRETT,
FREDDIE GORMAN and BRIAN HOLLAND

min - ute, Mis - ter Post - man.)   (Wait.)   (Wait a
Please, _____ Mis - ter Post - man.

min - ute, Mis - ter Post - man.) De - liv - er de let - ter,   the

soon - er de bet - ter.

Optional Ending

Repeat ad lib. and Fade

REACH OUT AND TOUCH
(Somebody's Hand)

Words and Music by NICKOLAS ASHFORD
and VALERIE SIMPSON

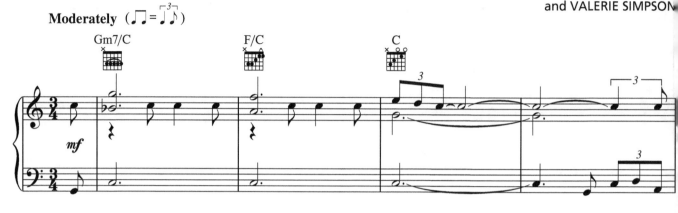

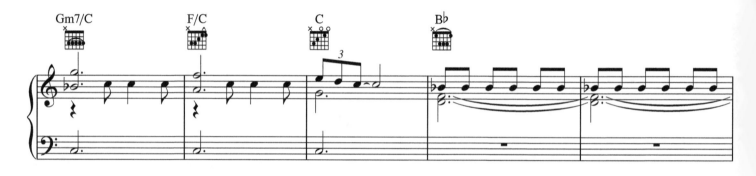

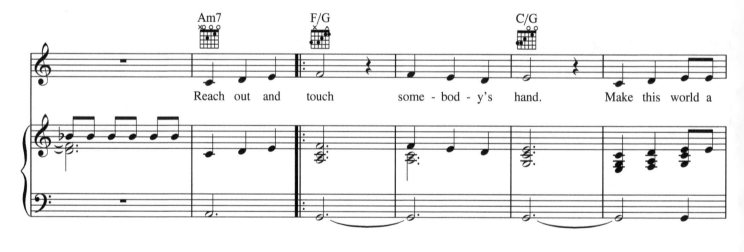

Reach out and touch some-bod-y's hand. Make this world a

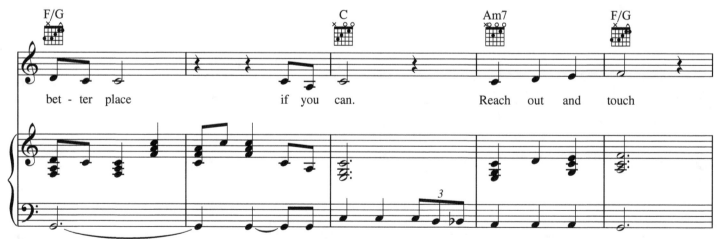

bet - ter place if you can. Reach out and touch

REACH OUT, I'LL BE THERE

Words and Music by BRIAN HOLLAND,
LAMONT DOZIER and EDWARD HOLLAND

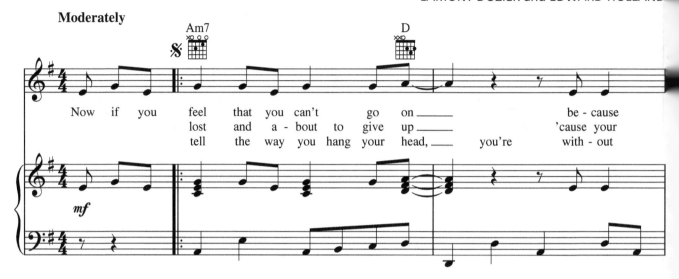

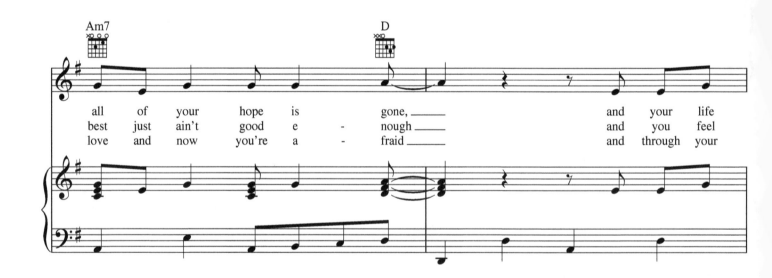

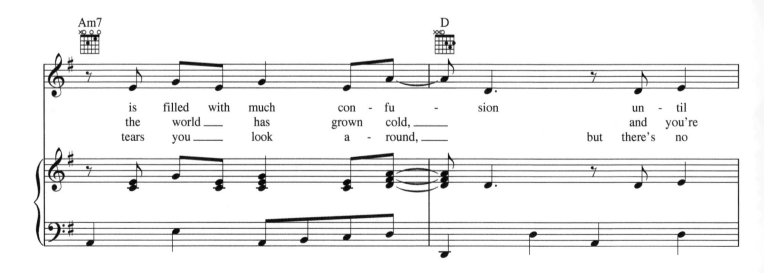

with a love ___ that will shel - ter you. _____
to love ___ and com - fort you, _____ and
to give you all the love you need, _____ and

I'll be there ___ with a love ___ that will see you through. _____
I'll be there ___ to cher - ish ___ and care for you. _____
I'll be there, ___ you can al - ways de - pend on me. _____ (Fade)

When you feel

I'll be there ___
I'll be there ___

to al - ways see you through. ___
to love and com - fort you. ___ I can

D.S. and Fade

SAIL ON

Words and Music by
LIONEL RICHIE

Sail on down _ the line _ 'bout a half a mile _ or so, _ and a
Sail on down _ the line. _ Ain't it fun-ny how the time _ can go _ on a

don't real - ly wan - na know a where you're go - in'. ____
friends say they told _ me so, _ but it does - n't mat - ter. ____

*Recorded a half step lower.

I guess I'll move a-long,___ I'm look-in' for a good_____ time,___

I want ev-er-y-one__ to know___ I'm look-in' for a good_____ time,___

___ good time,___

yeah.___

RIBBON IN THE SKY

Words and Music by
STEVIE WONDER

Slowly, with expression

Oh, so

SHOP AROUND

Words and Music by BERRY GORDY
and WILLIAM "SMOKEY" ROBINSON

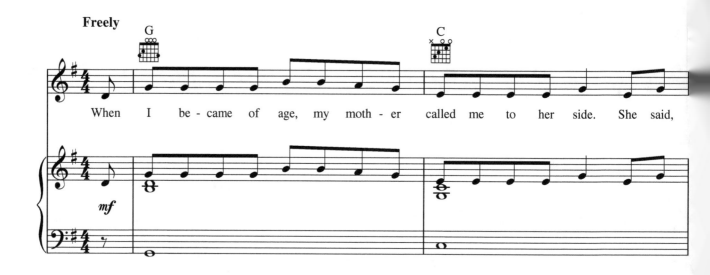

When I be-came of age, my moth-er called me to her side. She said,

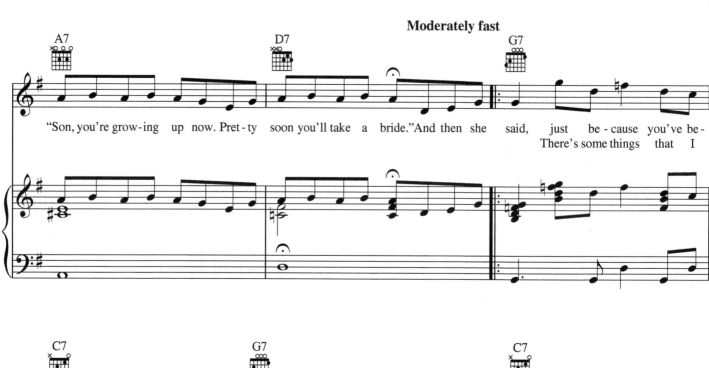

"Son, you're grow-ing up now. Pret-ty soon you'll take a bride." And then she said, just be-cause you've be-
There's some things that I

come a young man now, there's still some things that you don't un-der-stand now.
want you to know now. Just as sure as the wind's gon-na blow now,

Make sure that her love is true _ now, I hate to see you feel-in' sad _ and blue now. _

My ma-ma told me you bet-ter shop a - round. _

(Vocal 1st time only)

SHOT GUN

Words and Music
AUTRY DeWA

I said shot - gun.

go - in' down here lis - ten to ___ 'em play ___ the blues.   We're gon - na

dig po - ta - toes. ___   We're gon - na

pick to - ma - toes. ___   I said

shot - gun. _____

Shoot him 'fore he run now. Do the jerk, ba - by.

Do the jerk now. I said it's

cry - in' time. I said it's cry - in' time. Hey.

Repeat ad lib. and Fade

SOMEDAY WE'LL BE TOGETHER

Words and Music by JACKEY BEAVERS,
JOHNNY BRISTOL and HARVEY FUQUA

SIGNED, SEALED, DELIVERED I'M YOURS

Words and Music by STEVIE WONDER, SYREETA WRIGHT,
LEE GARRETT and LULA MAE HARDAWAY

Like a fool I went and stayed ____ too long. ____
Then that time I went and said ____ good - bye. ____
Seen a lot of things in this ____ old world. ____
Ooh - wee babe, you set my world ____ on fire. ____

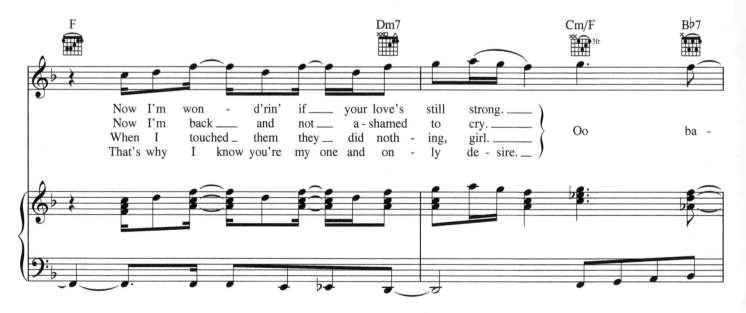

Now I'm won - d'rin' if ____ your love's still strong. ____
Now I'm back ____ and not ____ a - shamed to cry. ____
When I touched ____ them they ____ did noth - ing, girl. ____
That's why I know you're my one and on - ly de - sire. ____

Oo ba -

SIR DUKE

Words and Music by
STEVIE WONDER

Mu - sic is a world with - in it - self _____ with a
Mu - sic knows it is and al - ways will _____ be one of

lan - guage we all un - der - stand, _____
the things that life just won't quit. _____

SMILING FACES SOMETIMES

Words and Music by NORMAN WHITFIELD
and BARRETT STRONG

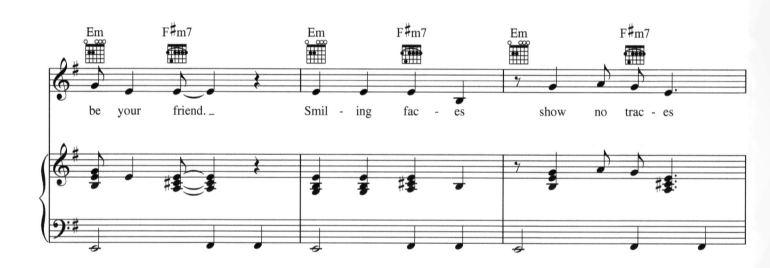

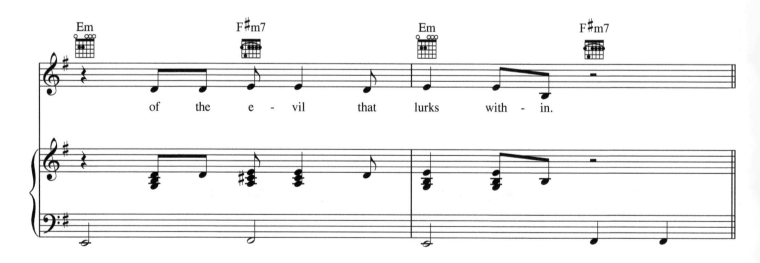

STILL

Words and Music
LIONEL RICH-

To Coda

Whispered: still.

rit.

a tempo

D.S. al Coda

We played the

CODA

STOP! IN THE NAME OF LOVE

Words and Music by LAMONT DOZIER
BRIAN HOLLAND and EDWARD HOLLAND

Stop! In the name of love,

be - fore you break my heart.

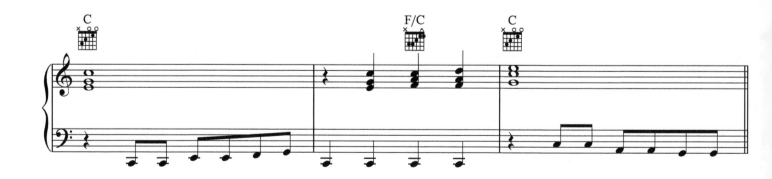

SUPER FREAK

Words and Music by RICK JAMES
and ALONZO MILLER

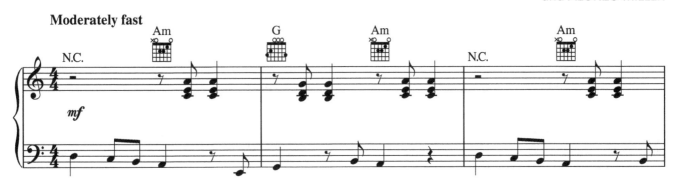

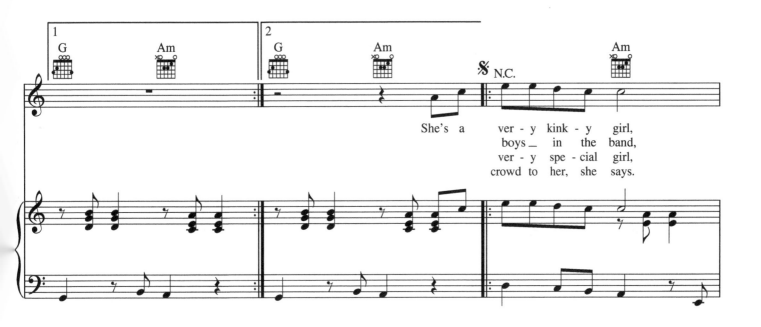

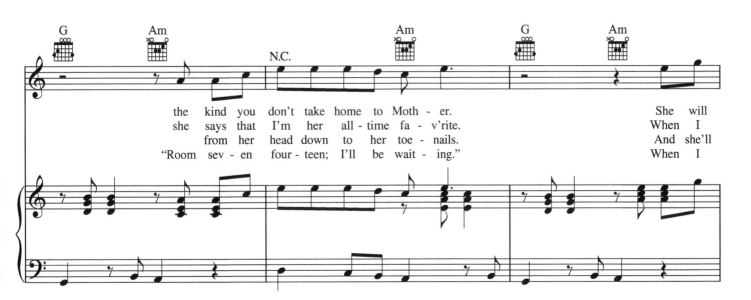

never let your spir - its down, _____ once you get her off___ the street.
make my move to her room, it's the right time; she's nev - er hard___ to please.
wait for me at back - stage with her girl - friends in a lim - ou - sine.
get there she's got in - cense, wine and can - dles; it's such a freak - y scene.

She likes the That girl is pret - ty wild ___ now. (The
Three's not a girl is pret - ty kink - y. (The

girl's a su - per freak.) The kind of girl you read a - bout (in
girl's a su - per freak.) I real - ly love to taste her

SUPERSTITION

Words and Music by
STEVIE WONDER

THE TEARS OF A CLOWN

Words and Music by STEVIE WONDER,
WILLIAM "SMOKEY" ROBINSON and HENRY COSBY

Additional Lyrics

Now, if there's a smile on my face
Don't let my glad expression
Give you a wrong impression
Don't let this smile I wear
Make you think that I don't care. *(Fade)*

WAR

Words and Music by NORMAN WHITFIELD
and BARRETT STRONG

Additional Lyrics

2. War, uh! What is it good for? Absolutely nothing; say it again;
   War, uh! What is it good for? Absolutely nothing.
   War, it's nothing but a heartbreaker; War, friend only to the undertaker.
   War is an enemy to all mankind. The thought of war blows my mind.
   War has caused unrest within the younger generation;
   Induction then destruction, who wants to die? Ah
   War, uh um; What is it good for? You tell me nothing, um!
   War, uh! What is it good for? Absolutely nothing.
   Good God, war, it's nothing but a heartbreaker;
   War, friend only to the undertaker;

3. Wars have shattered many a young man's dreams;
   Made him disabled, bitter and mean.
   Life is much too short and precious to spend fighting wars each day.
   War can't give life, it can only take it away. Ah
   War, Uh um! What is it good for? Absolutely nothing, um.
   War, good God almighty, listen, what is it good for? Absolutely nothing, yeah.
   War, it's nothing but a heartbreaker; War, friend only to the undertaker.
   Peace, love and understanding, tell me is there no place for them today?
   They say we must fight to keep our freedom, but Lord knows it's gotta be a better way.
   I say war, uh um, yeah, yeah. What is it good for? Absolutely nothing; say it again;
   War, yea, yea, yea, yea, what is it good for? Absolutely nothing; say it again;
   War, nothing but a heartbreaker; What is it good for? Friend only to the undertaker....
   (Fade)

THREE TIMES A LADY

Words and Music by
LIONEL RICHI

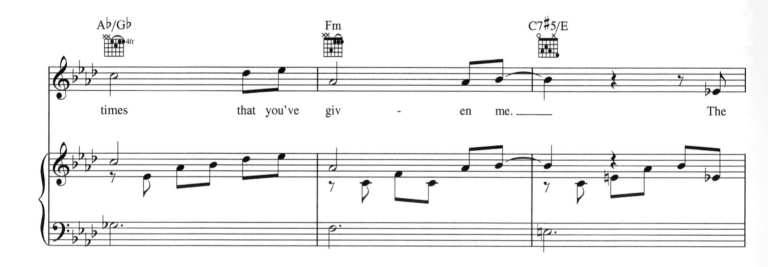

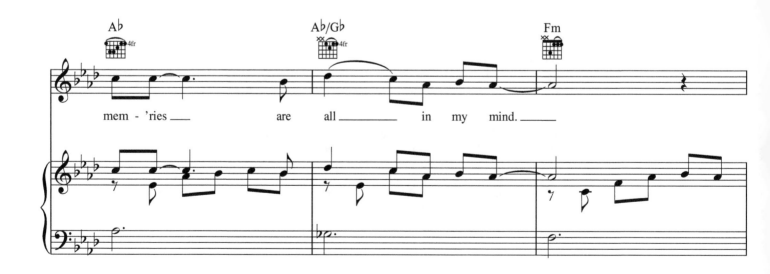

TOO BUSY THINKING
ABOUT MY BABY

Words and Music by JANIE BRADFORD,
NORMAN WHITFIELD and BARRETT STRONG

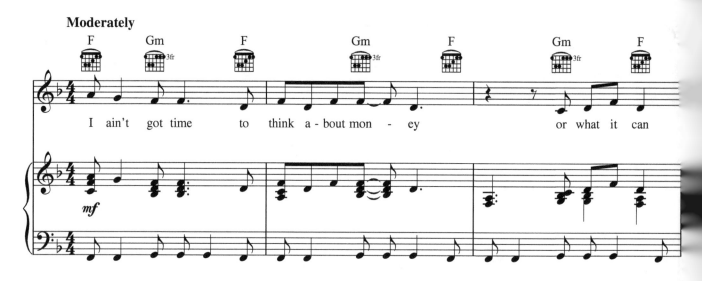

I ain't got time to think a-bout mon—ey or what it can

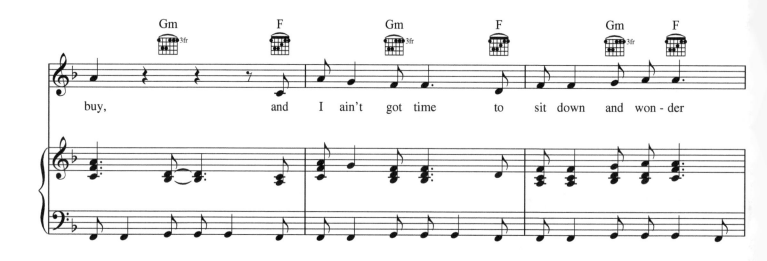

buy, and I ain't got time to sit down and won-der

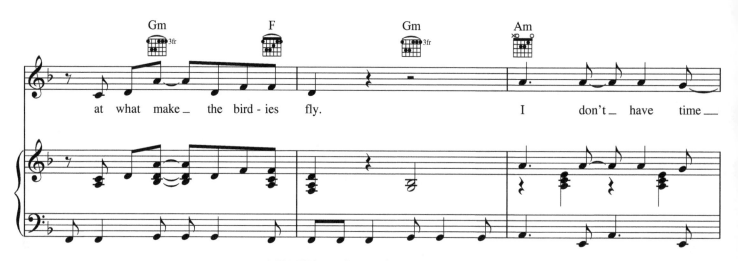

at what make_ the bird-ies fly. I don't_ have time

TOUCH ME IN THE MORNING

Words and Music by RONALD MILLE
and MICHAEL MASSE

THE TRACKS OF MY TEARS

Words and Music by WILLIAM "SMOKEY" ROBINSON
WARREN MOORE and MARVIN TARPLIN

TRULY

Words and Music by
LIONEL RICHIE

UPTIGHT
(Everything's Alright)

Words and Music by STEVIE WOND
SYLVIA MOY and HENRY COS

THE WAY YOU DO THE THINGS YOU DO

Words and Music by WILLIAM "SMOKEY" ROBINSON
and ROBERT ROGERS

broom. _ / cool crook.

The way you smell so sweet, / And, ba - by, you're so smart,

you know you could -'ve been some / you know you could -'ve been a

per - fume. _ / school book. _

Well, __ you could -'ve been an - y - thing that you

want - ed to and I can tell. _

The way you do the things you do. _ Ah, ba -

- by.

As pret - ty as you

- by.

Yes! __

WHAT BECOMES OF THE BROKEN HEARTED

Words and Music by JAMES A. DEAN
PAUL RISER and WILLIAM HENRY WEATHERSPOON

Moderately

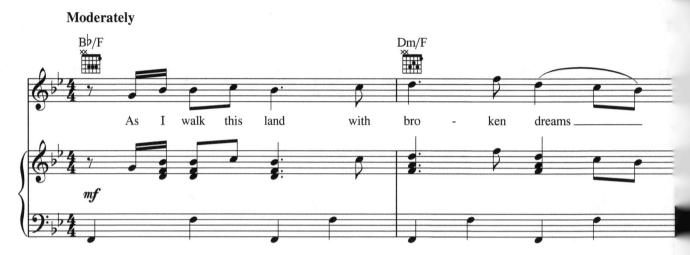

As I walk this land with bro - ken dreams ___

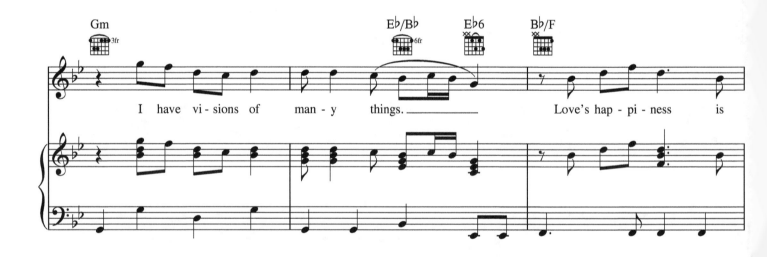

I have vi - sions of man - y things. ___ Love's hap - pi - ness is

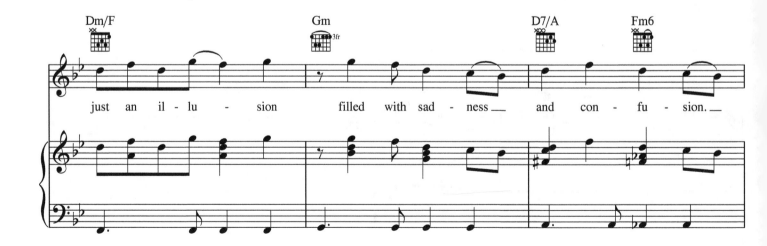

just an il - lu - sion filled with sad - ness ___ and con - fu - sion. ___

WHAT DOES IT TAKE
(To Win Your Love)

Words and Music by JOHN BRISTOL
VERNON BULLOCK and HARVEY FUQU...

WHAT'S GOING ON

Words and Music by RENALDO BENSON
ALFRED CLEVELAND and MARVIN GAYE

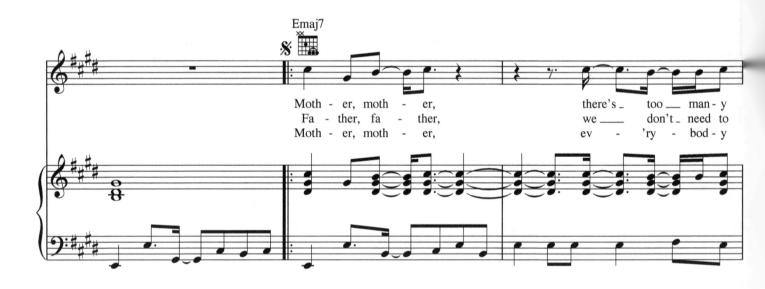

Moth - er, moth - er, there's _ too _ man - y
Fa - ther, fa - ther, we _ don't _ need to
Moth - er, moth - er, ev - 'ry - bod - y

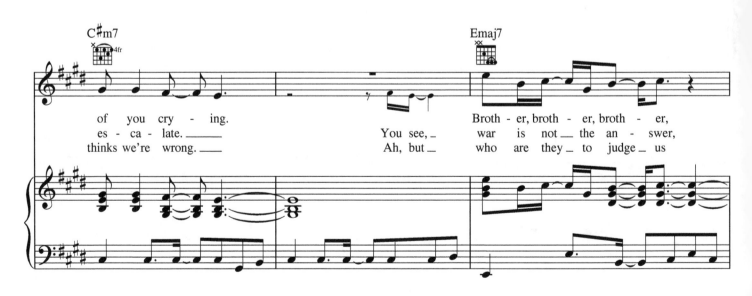

of you cry - ing.
es - ca - late. _
thinks we're wrong. _

You see, _ war is not _ the an - swer,
Ah, but _ who are they _ to judge _ us

Broth - er, broth - er, broth - er,

422

WHERE DID OUR LOVE GO

Words and Music by BRIAN HOLLAND
LAMONT DOZIER and EDWARD HOLLAND

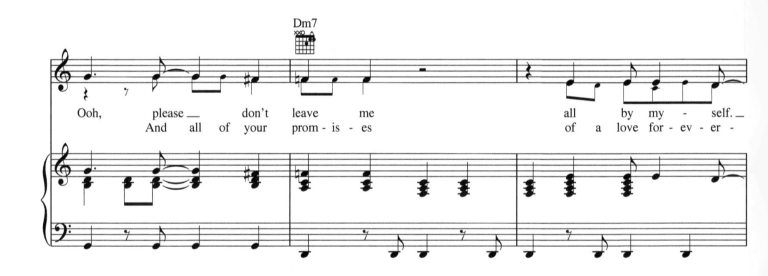

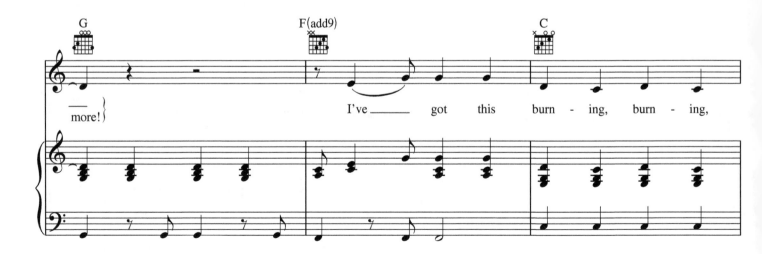

YESTER-ME, YESTER-YOU, YESTERDAY

Words by RON MILLER
Music by BRYAN WELLS

Moderately

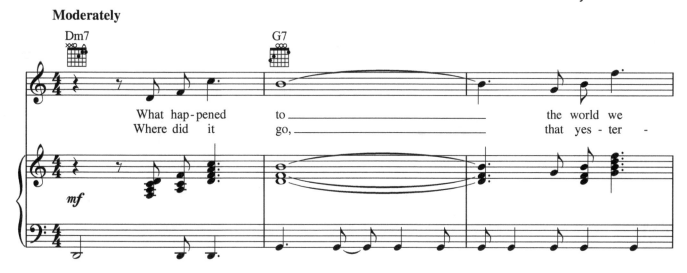

What hap-pened to ___ the world we
Where did it go, ___ that yes - ter -

knew, when we would dream and scheme and
glow, when we could feel the wheel and of

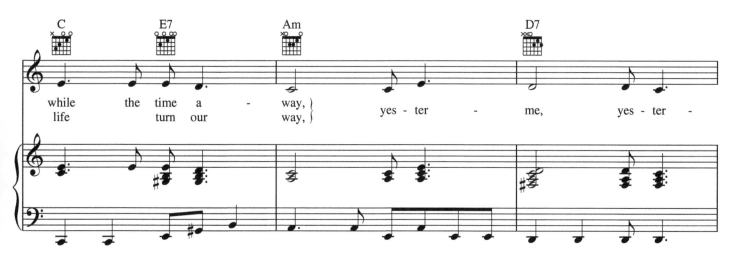

while the time a - way, } yes - ter - me, yes - ter -
life turn our way, } yes - ter -

YOU AND I

Words and Music by
STEVIE WONDER

Here we are on earth to-geth-er it's you and I.
I am glad at least in my life I found some-one

God has made us fall in love, it's true. I've
that may not be here for-ev-er to see me through. But

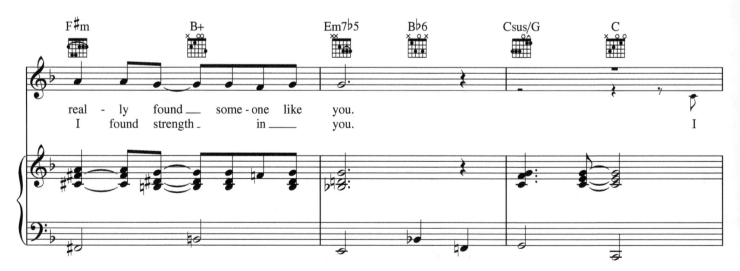

real-ly found some-one like you.
I found strength in you.
I

Will it stay, the love you feel for me? Will it say
on - ly pray that I have shown you a bright - er day,

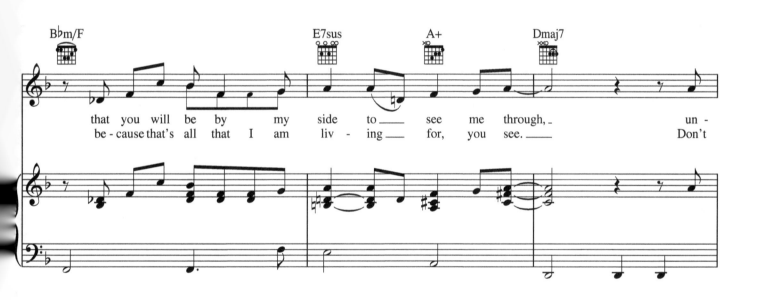

that you will be by my side to ___ see me through, ___ un -
be - cause that's all that I am liv - ing ___ for, you see. ___ Don't

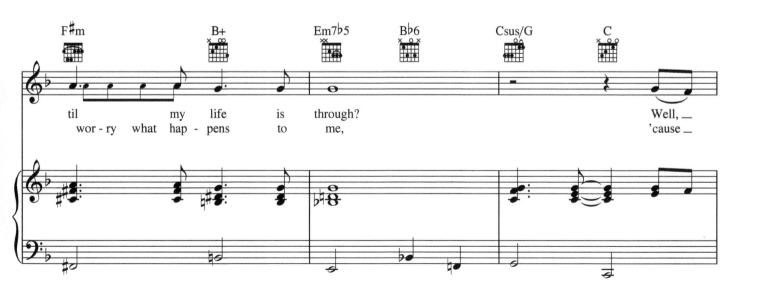

til my life is through? Well, __
wor - ry what hap - pens to me, 'cause __

YOU ARE THE SUNSHINE OF MY LIFE

Words and Music by
STEVIE WONDER

YOU CAN'T HURRY LOVE

Words and Music by EDWARD HOLLAND,
LAMONT DOZIER and BRIAN HOLLAND

439

YOU KEEP ME HANGIN' ON

Words and Music by EDWARD HOLLAND,
LAMONT DOZIER and BRIAN HOLLAND

* Recorded a half step lower.

YOU'RE ALL I NEED TO GET BY

Words and Music by NICKOLAS ASHFO...
and VALERIE SIMPS...

You're all   I   need   to get

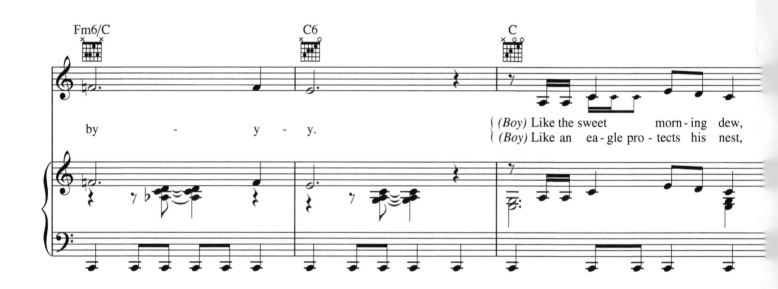

by -   y - y.

{ (Boy) Like the sweet   morn-ing dew,
{ (Boy) Like an ea-gle pro-tects his nest,

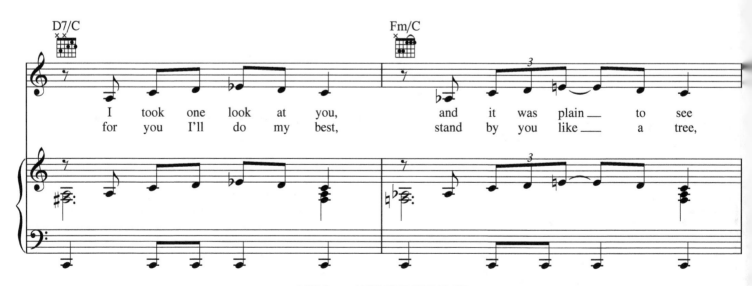

I   took   one   look at   you,   and it was plain __ to see
for you   I'll   do   my best,   stand by you like __ a tree,

D7   **Fm**

(Boy) And when I ___ lose my will ___ you'll be there ___ to push me up the hill. ___ There's
(Boy) I know you ___ can make a man out of a soul ___ that did-n't have a goal. ___ 'Cause

C   **F**   **C**   **F**

no   no look-ing back ___ for us, ___
we,   we got the right ___ foun-da-   tion

C   **F6**   **C**   **D7**   **Fm**

we got love ___ sure 'nough, ___ that's e-nough. ___ You're
and with love ___ and de-ter- mi-na-tion. ___ You're

1
C   **F**   **C**   **Fm**   **C**   **Fm**   **G7♭5**

all,   you're all I need ___ to get by. ___   I

YOU'VE REALLY GOT A HOLD ON ME

Words and Music by
WILLIAM "SMOKEY" ROBINSON

Slowly

I don't ____ like you, ____ but I ____ love you;
I don't ____ want you, ____ but I ____ need you;
I wan - na leave you, ____ don't wan - na stay here;

seems that I'm al - ways ____ think - ing of you. ____
don't wan - na kiss you, ____ but I ____ need to. ____
don't wan - na spend _____ an - oth - er day here. ____

YOU'VE MADE ME SO VERY HAPPY

Words and Music by BERRY GORDY, FRANK E. WILSON
BRENDA HOLLOWAY and PATRICE HOLLOWAY

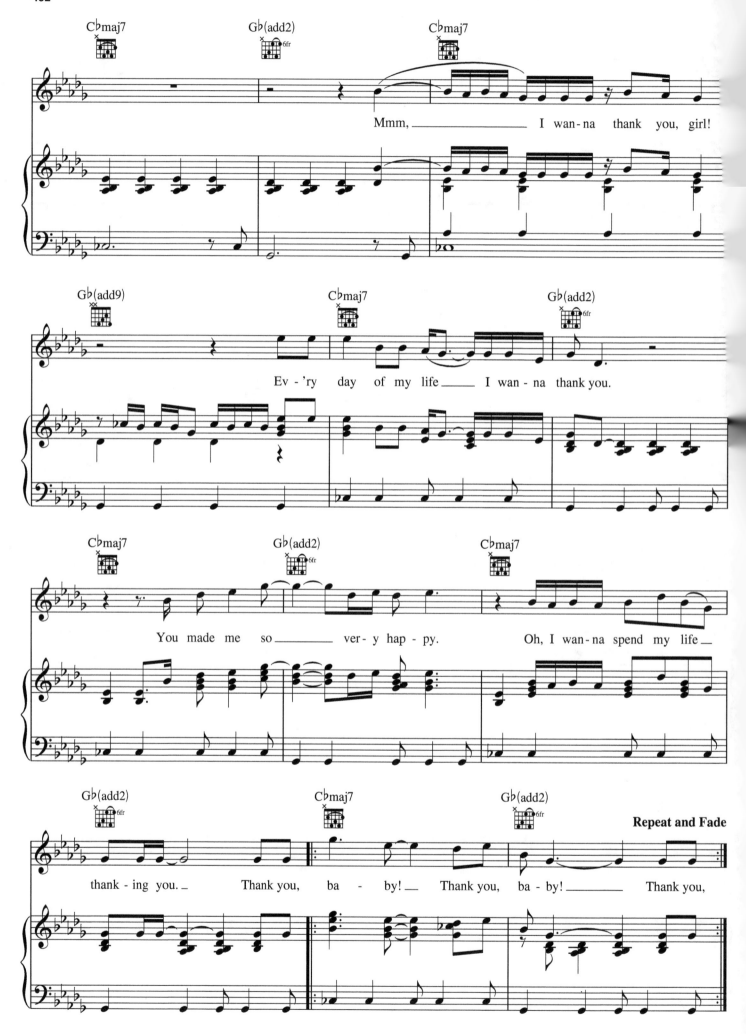